3 4028 07639 1136
HARRIS COUNTY PUBLIC LIBRARY

J 395.122 Man
Manners mash-up : a goofy
guide to good behavior

$16.99
ocn535490588
02/23/2011

D0116212

WITHDRAWN

Featuring:

TEDD ARNOLD
JOE BERGER
SOPHIE BLACKALL
HENRY COLE
FRANK MORRISON
LYNN MUNSINGER
TAO NYEU
LEUYEN PHAM
ADAM REX
PETER H. REYNOLDS
DAN SANTAT
JUDY SCHACHNER
BOB SHEA
and KEVIN SHERRY

MANNERS MASH-UP

A GOOFY GUIDE to GOOD BEHAVIOR

DIAL BOOKS FOR YOUNG READERS

an imprint of Penguin Group (USA) Inc.

DIAL BOOKS FOR YOUNG READERS

A DIVISION OF PENGUIN YOUNG READERS GROUP · PUBLISHED BY THE PENGUIN GROUP

Penguin Group (USA) Inc., 375 Hudson Street, New York, NY 10014, U.S.A.

Penguin Group (Canada), 90 Eglinton Avenue East, Suite 700, Toronto, Ontario, Canada M4P 2Y3
(a division of Pearson Penguin Canada Inc.) · Penguin Books Ltd, 80 Strand, London WC2R 0RL,
England · Penguin Ireland, 25 St. Stephen's Green, Dublin 2, Ireland (a division of Penguin Books Ltd)
Penguin Group (Australia), 250 Camberwell Road, Camberwell, Victoria 3124, Australia (a division of Pearson
Australia Group Pty Ltd) · Penguin Books India Pvt Ltd, 11 Community Centre, Panchsheel Park, New Delhi - 110
017, India · Penguin Group (NZ), 67 Apollo Drive, Rosedale, North Shore 0632, New Zealand (a division of Pearson New
Zealand Ltd) · Penguin Books (South Africa) (Pty) Ltd, 24 Sturdee Avenue, Rosebank, Johannesburg 2196, South Africa
Penguin Books Ltd, Registered Offices: 80 Strand, London WC2R 0RL, England

Pages 8–9 © 2011 by Bob Shea
Pages 10–11 © 2011 by Lynn Munsinger
Pages 12–13 © 2011 by Henry Cole
Pages 14–15 © 2011 by LeUyen Pham
Pages 16–17 © 2011 by Peter H. Reynolds
Pages 18–19 © 2011 by Tedd Arnold
Pages 20–21 © 2011 by Adam Rex
Pages 22–23 © 2011 by Judith Byron Schachner
Pages 24–25 © 2011 by Frank Morrison
Pages 26–27 © 2011 by Sophie Blackall
Pages 28–29 © 2011 by Dan Santat
Pages 30–31 © 2011 by Joe Berger
Pages 32–33 © 2011 by Kevin Sherry
Pages 34–35 © 2011 by Tao Nyeu
All rights reserved

Library of Congress Cataloging-in-Publication Data
Manners mash-up: a goofy guide to good behavior :
featuring Tedd Arnold ... [et al.].
p. cm.
ISBN 978-0-8037-3480-7 (hardcover)
1. Etiquette for children and teenagers—Humor.
I. Arnold, Tedd.
BJ1857.C5M125 2010
395.1'22—dc22
2010011882

The publisher does not have any control over and does not
assume any responsibility for author or third-party
websites or their content.

The illustrations in this book are the copyrighted property of the respective illustrator.
Designed by Jennifer Kelly
Manufactured in China on acid-free paper

1 3 5 7 9 10 8 6 4 2

Say please!

TURN THE PAGE
* TO FIND: *

Bob Shea on the SCHOOL BUS

Lynn Munsinger in the CAFETERIA

Henry Cole with a STARING PROBLEM

LeUyen Pham on the PLAYGROUND

Peter H. Reynolds in the CLASSROOM

Tedd Arnold on SPORTSMANSHIP

Adam Rex at the DINNER TABLE

Judy Schachner at a BIRTHDAY PARTY

Frank Morrison VISITING RELATIVES

Sophie Blackall at the DOCTOR'S OFFICE

Dan Santat at the THEATER

Joe Berger at the SUPERMARKET

Kevin Sherry at the SWIMMING POOL

Tao Nyeu at a "PICK"-NIC

BUS MANNERS

NO DANCING

DON'T EAVESDROP

DON'T PRACTICE YOUR TROMBONE

DON'T WORK ON YOUR SCIENCE PROJECT

DON'T SOAK YOUR SEATMATE WITH SLEEP DROOL

SAY "excuse me" WHEN YOU MAKE A SMELL

Don't hog the ball

Wait your turn!

No throwing sand
in the sandbox

art by
LeUYen Pham

Classroom Manners

art by PETER H. REYNOLDS

GOOD SPORTS
PARKING SPACE
THE ALL-ALIEN SLIMEBALL CHAMPIONSHIP
NEWS
WELCOME, SPORTS FANS! TODAY WE'RE EXPECTING **WILD** ACTION DOWN IN THE OL' SLIME PIT. BUT FIRST, A FEW REMINDERS...
art by TEDD ARNOLD

TABLE MANNERS
Don't talk with your mouth full.
And no elbows or feet on the table.
And Igor— don't slouch.
art by ADAM REX

Be a Good Visitor

art by FRANK MORRISON

Manners

Help out if you're asked

Don't make a mess

Give a polite greeting

Don't insult the host

Keep your feet off
the furniture

Don't play ball in
the house

PLEASE DON'T PICK YOUR NOSE AND LEAVE THE BOOGERS UNDER THE SEAT. THAT SPOT IS SAVED FOR OLD CHEWED GUM WADS ONLY. YUMMY! YUMMY!

PLEASE LEAVE THE PORTABLE GAME SYSTEM AT HOME. RIDDING THE GALAXY OF EVIL ALIENS CAN WAIT UNTIL AFTER YOU LEAVE.

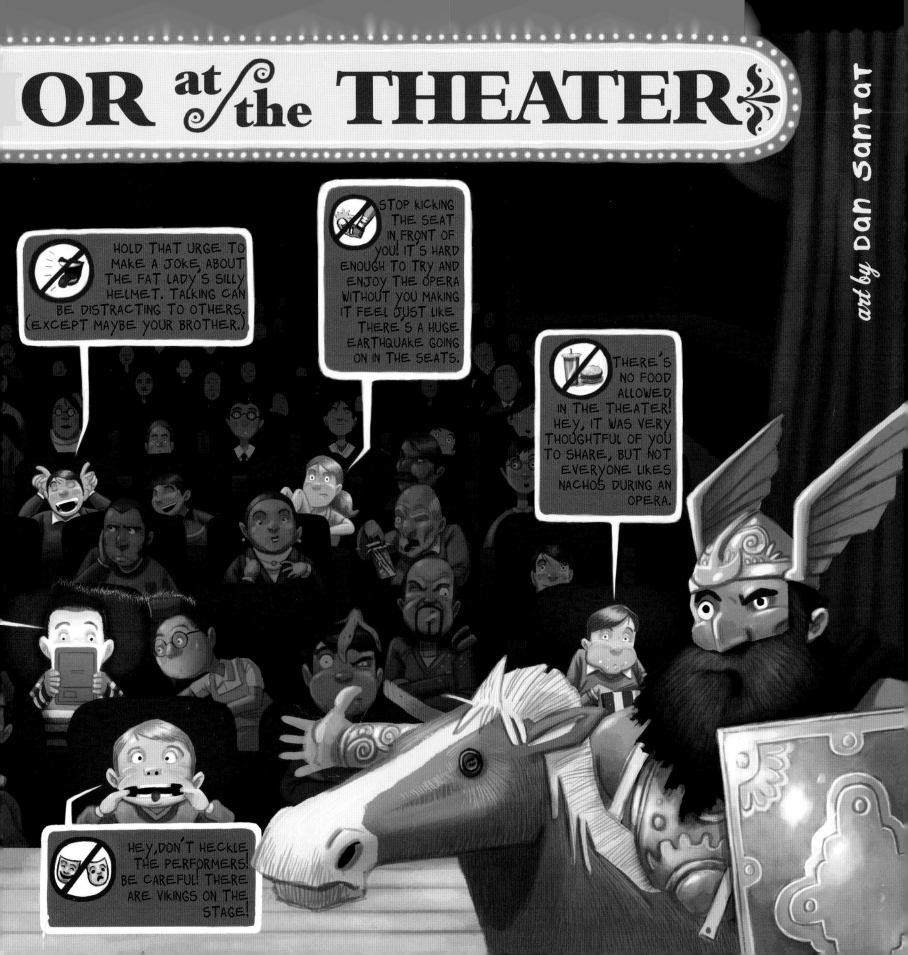

WHat Was YOUR GOOFIEST

WINGS!

When I was little, I had a very bad habit of hunching over the table, sticking my elbows out, and waggling them up and down while eating, rather than sitting up straight with my arms down at my sides. My elbows would prod my sister on one side, and my mum or dad on the other. My dad would shout "Wings!" which was my cue to sit up properly and fold my wings down.

Joe Berger's books include:
Bridget Fidget and the Most Perfect Pet!; *Hattie the Bad*

It's good manners to have your fly zipped up, right? I had very bad manners for an entire day in the spring of 1985.

© Sonya Sones

Adam Rex's books include:
Frankenstein Makes a Sandwich; *Frankenstein Takes the Cake*; *Guess Again!* by Mac Barnett

When I was a kid, I used to draw portraits of the other students. One day, someone asked me to draw the teacher. So I did. A scribble here, a line there, a box for a head, a carrot for a nose, waffle ears, the teacher's name at the top, and just like that I was done. Little did I know, but my teacher was standing there the whole time.

Frank Morrison's books include:
the Keena Ford series by Melissa Thomson; *The Hat That Wore Clara B.* by Melanie Turner-Denstaedt; *For the Love of Soccer!* by Pelé

I didn't show up to a surprise birthday party for a friend . . . and I was the one giving the party!

Henry Cole's books include:
A Nest for Celeste; *On Meadowview Street*; Big Chickens series by Leslie Helakoski

Kevin Sherry blows his nose REALLY loudly, like an elephant. He can't help it. On the first day of school, he would blow his nose in front of the whole class. The other kids would laugh, but then realize that was just how he sounded, and wouldn't laugh for the rest of the year.

Kevin Sherry's books include:
I'm the Biggest Thing in the Ocean; *I'm the Best Artist in the Ocean*; *Acorns Everywhere!*

One day at lunchtime I rushed to an art show. I was going to be the judge. I wolfed down a hamburger on the way. At the art gallery I acted like a sophisticated judge of art. I thought I was cool! Later, I found a huge, gross smear of mustardy ketchup on my shirt. Not so cool! Never wolf down your food.

Tedd Arnold's books include:
Hi! Fly Guy; *Green Wilma, Frog in Space*; *Parts*

I once told Santa that the present he gave me at the school Christmas party was stinky. I got a packet of hair bands, when anyone could see I had short hair. My mother made me go to Santa and apologize.

Sophie Blackall's books include:
the Ivy and Bean series by Annie Barrows; *Big Red Lollipop* by Rukhsana Khan; *Wombat Walkabout* by Carol Diggory Shields

manners mishap?

UYEN AT WORK

LeUyen Pham (pronounced "Lay Win Fam") falls asleep everywhere. She is known to fall asleep while other people are talking to her, within the first ten minutes of any movie, when talking for more then twenty minutes on the phone, during any meeting, and once, she nearly fell asleep during a speech that someone else was making about her. Other than that, LeUyen has VERY good manners.

LeUyen Pham's books include: *Freckleface Strawberry* by Julianne Moore; *God's Dream* by Archbishop Desmond Tutu; *Big Sister, Little Sister*

Lynn Munsinger's books include: *Skunks!* by David T. Greenberg; *What Sisters Do Best/What Brothers Do Best* by Laura Numeroff; *The Underground Gators* by Tina Casey

I accidentally picked my nose while posing for this portrait!

Tao Nyeu's books include: *Wonder Bear; Bunny Days*

I was on a trip to China. Our group was treated to an elaborate banquet with many courses, including some rather unfamiliar delicacies like jellyfish tentacles. There were a lot of different little bowls set out with sauces. All of a sudden our horrified hosts ran up and pointed out that we Americans were busily dipping our food into the finger bowls. I do remember thinking that that was a rather bland sauce!

SLOP

One time there was a dusty western town full of dusty townspeople. Some bad men came and started bossing everyone around.
A mysterious stranger (me!) rode into town and said, "Hey you bad men, stop being so bossy!"
The bad men said, "Why don't you make us?"
"Because I don't make monkeys!" I said.
They knew I was serious, because they got on their horses and bikes and ran away.
As I rode out of town the dusty townspeople looked at my silhouette against the orange sunset and said, "We didn't even get a chance to thank him!"
Which was totally rude of me.

Bob Shea's books include: *Oh, Daddy!; Race you to Bed; Dinosaur vs. Bedtime*

It was my birthday and I could cry if I wanted—which I did every time someone sang the birthday song to me.

Judy Schachner's books include: *Skippyjon Jones; The Grannyman; Yo, Vikings!*

One day I was walking through Harvard Square in Cambridge when a rather cute girl came running at me full tilt, grabbed me, gave me a great big squeezy hug, and then planted a big, sloppy kiss on me. I had NO idea who this girl was! As she pulled back from me and saw my stunned face, she said, "Oh my gosh! Paul said he had a twin brother! I am soooo sorry!!" I politely replied, "Please—don't worry! These things happen," and walked away smiling ear to ear.

PETER H. REYNOLDS

Peter H. Reynolds's books include: *Huck Runs Amuck!* by Sean Taylor; *Rose's Garden; The North Star*

My parents told me that when I was very little (maybe one or two years old), when we were in restaurants I would eat chicken and then throw the bones at the other customers sitting in their seats. True story.

BURP!

Dan Santat's books include: *Always Lots of Heinies at the Zoo* by Ayun Halliday; *Chicken Dance* by Tammi Sauer; *The Secret Life of Walter Kitty* by Barbara Jean Hicks

Harris County Public Library
Houston, Texas

WITHDRAWN
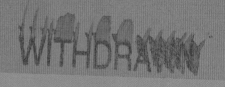